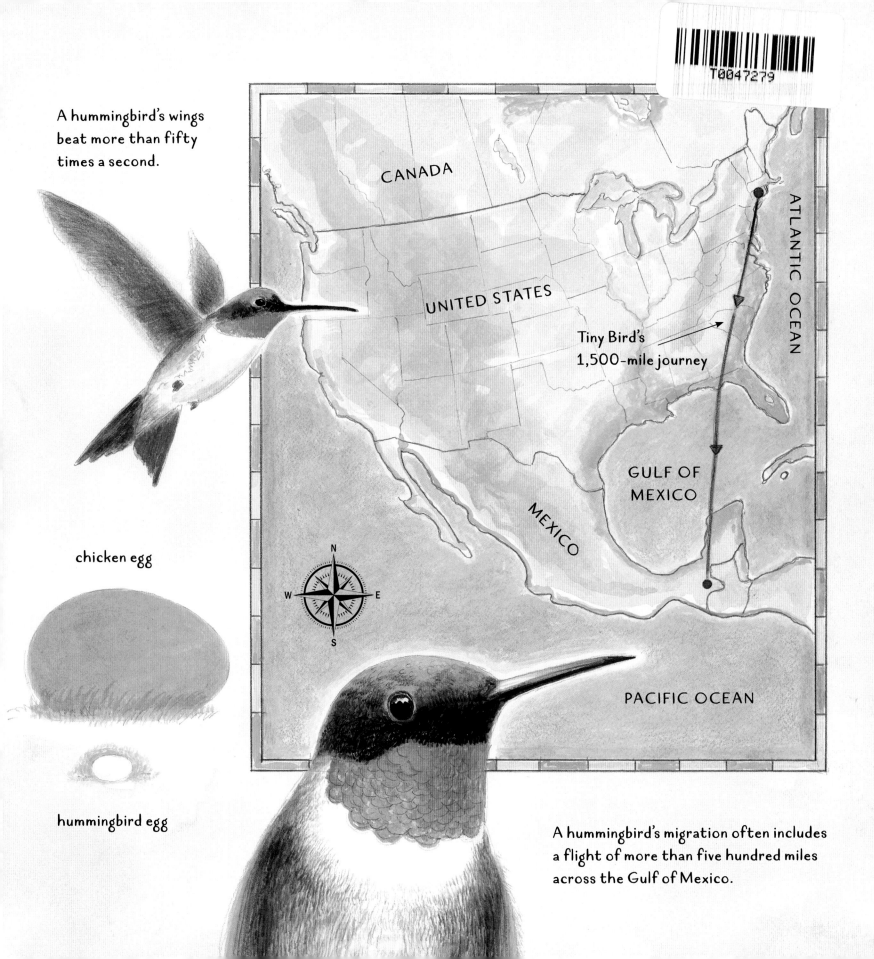

A hummingbird's wings beat more than fifty times a second.

chicken egg

hummingbird egg

CANADA

UNITED STATES

Tiny Bird's
1,500-mile journey

ATLANTIC OCEAN

GULF OF
MEXICO

MEXICO

PACIFIC OCEAN

A hummingbird's migration often includes
a flight of more than five hundred miles
across the Gulf of Mexico.

For Felix, Graham, Lulu,
and Evan. Keep flying high!
—R. B.

To my friend Evie Chang Henderson
—W. M.

Henry Holt and Company, *Publishers since 1866*
Henry Holt® is a registered trademark of Macmillan Publishing Group, LLC
120 Broadway, New York, NY 10271 · mackids.com

Library of Congress Cataloging-in-Publication Data
Names: Burleigh, Robert, author. | Minor, Wendell, illustrator. Title: Tiny Bird : a hummingbird's amazing journey / Robert Burleigh ;
illustrated by Wendell Minor. Description: First edition. | New York : Christy Ottaviano Books, Henry Holt and Company, 2020. | Summary:
As autumn nears, flowers fade and insects become quiet, and Tiny Bird leaves his northern home for the long and perilous journey to lush
southern forests. Includes facts about hummingbirds. Identifiers: LCCN 2019018544 | ISBN 9781627793698 (hardcover : alk. paper)
Subjects: LCSH: Ruby-throated hummingbird—Juvenile fiction. | CYAC: Ruby-throated hummingbird—Fiction. | Hummingbirds—Fiction. |
Birds—Migration—Fiction. Classification: LCC PZ10.3.B87 Tin 2020 | DDC [E]—dc23
LC record available at https://lccn.loc.gov/2019018544

Our books may be purchased in bulk for promotional, educational, or business use. Please contact your local bookseller or the Macmillan
Corporate and Premium Sales Department at (800) 221-7945 ext. 5442 or by email at MacmillanSpecialMarkets@macmillan.com.

First edition, 2020 / Designed by Vera Soki
The artist used gouache watercolor on Strathmore 500 Bristol paper to create the illustrations for this book.
Printed in China by RR Donnelley Asia Printing Solutions Ltd.,
Dongguan City, Guangdong Province

3 5 7 9 10 8 6 4 2

Tiny Bird

A Hummingbird's Amazing Journey

ROBERT BURLEIGH   ILLUSTRATED BY WENDELL MINOR

Christy Ottaviano Books
Henry Holt and Company
New York

Today is the day.

In the yard,
the last orange flowers
open their petals to the slanting sun.

A tiny ruby-throated hummingbird is feeding.
Just three inches long,
Tiny Bird hovers above a blossom
as if hanging from an unseen thread.

Whir!

Its wings flutter more than fifty times a second—so rapidly they're nearly invisible.

Zip!

It darts up.

Zap!

It flits down.

Flower to flower,
backward, forward, under, over,
like an acrobat of the air!

Radiant green feathers glimmering,
ruby throat shimmering,
Tiny Bird delicately dips its beak
into the heart of each flower,
extracting precious nectar.
It will need as much food as it can gather
for the hard trip ahead.

The flowers are fading. Insects grow quiet.
Leaves are turning yellow.
Autumn is coming.
Born in this northeastern yard,
Tiny Bird has explored every inch of its small territory.
But now it feels a pull and knows it must go.
It must leave this familiar place
and fly to a far-off winter home.

Today is the day.

Away!
Heading south all alone,
Tiny Bird begins its amazing journey.

It flies low, skimming the tops of trees.
Zoom! Its wings rapidly rotating,

Tiny Bird speeds along—
sometimes nearly thirty miles an hour.
No one sees it gliding over farms, fields, train tracks,
smokestacks, houses, and schools.
But Tiny Bird sees everything—
its eyes are sharp.

Diving down, it spots a few flowers
on which to feed.

Jab! Poke!

Flicking sideways,
it snatches a passing fly
and even raids a spiderweb—
more fuel for its long trip.

Whoops—danger!
Quickly, Tiny Bird zigzags
out of the path of a hawk,
reeling from the **whoosh**
of the hawk's enormous wings.

A close call!

Day after day, farther and farther,
pausing to rest here and there along the way,
Tiny Bird travels southward.
And yet it must keep going.
The most difficult part of its perilous journey
is soon to come.

The Gulf of Mexico lies waiting.
Dark blue, deep, and vast,
it glitters in the sun.

Tiny Bird lingers for a moment near the shore,
its tongue unfurling to gather flower nectar.
Quicker than a blink, it nabs one last mosquito.

Then—into the air!
Over the first pounding waves,
it begins its nonstop flight of more than twenty hours.
Can Tiny Bird make it?
Many hummingbirds never do.

As far as the distant horizon,
there is nothing but sky and sea.
An empty expanse of water
stretches in all directions.
Tiny Bird makes its way,
staying just inside the curves of the waves
to protect itself from the onrushing wind.

Watch out!
A fish leaps up,
its jaws snapping,
narrowly missing the little bird.

As the setting sun tints the sky orange,
dark clouds form.
A sudden storm stirs up the sea.
Between flashes of lightning,
Tiny Bird struggles, fighting through
the wind and pelting rain.
Thunder crashes. Ba-boom!

Slower. Slower.
Tiny Bird begins to falter.
Its wings grow heavy as it dips
ever closer to the dangerous water.

Finally, the wind dies down.
The storm moves on.
In the darkness ahead,
a small fishing boat rocks,
its dim light swaying.
A resting place!
Tiny Bird perches lightly
on the bow of the wooden boat,
gathering strength.
Then—into the night again!

Marbled clouds pass.
Moonlight opens
a smooth and widening path
on the water.
Millions of stars blanket the sky.
At last, Earth's horizon glimmers
with the first hint of day.

Suddenly—
in the dawn light,
above a wave's curl—
land!

Green trees and vines!
Rainbow-hued flowers!
Tiny Bird is worn and thin after its travels.
Exhausted, it rests on a twig
for precious seconds.
Then it flits into the forest
to feed on plentiful flowers and insects.

Today is the day.
After flying more than 1,500 miles,
Tiny Bird has arrived.
It has reached its winter home at last.

In the spring, it will return,
flying back to the same yard
it left so many months earlier.
But for now,
Tiny Bird rests and feeds,
flickering from flower to flower
like an emerald spark flashing in the bright sun.

Yes, today is the day!

Fun Facts About Hummingbirds

Many Kinds of Hummingbirds

There are many different kinds, or species, of hummingbirds. All of them live in the Americas: North, Central, or South. The ruby-throated hummingbird—named for the ruby-red marking on the male's chest—is the most common hummingbird in the United States.

That Beautiful Bird

The first Europeans to come to the Americas had never seen hummingbirds. But the Spanish soon gave them a special name: *joyas voladoras*, "flying jewels."

How Tiny?

Some species of hummingbirds are the smallest birds in the world. A fully grown ruby-throated hummingbird is about as big as an adult's thumb. And it weighs only as much as a penny.

Really, Really Tiny

A mother hummingbird typically lays two eggs, each of which is about the size of a pea. The female hummingbird builds the nest, usually located on a tree branch and made of twigs and leaves. The eggs hatch in about two weeks, and the mother feeds the tiny birds until they are ready to fly. Then the young birds take off and don't return to their nest.

Who Needs a Nest?

Not grown hummingbirds. So where and how do they sleep? Hummingbirds sleep on a branch while standing on their thin legs. When they wake, off they go again.

Winging It

A hummingbird needs to rotate its wings rapidly to fly in many directions. How fast do they move? The wings of a ruby-throated hummingbird vibrate more than fifty times per second. That's so fast you can barely see them!

A Little Bird with a Big Appetite

A ruby-throated hummingbird eats about every ten to fifteen minutes throughout the day. It feasts on insects and flower nectar (or nectar substitutes from a human-made feeder). A hummingbird, with its sharp eyes and quick movements, catches and consumes more than three hundred insects a day.

No Sniffing Here

Hummingbirds have no sense of smell. Instead, they identify flowers by sight. They seek out brightly colored flowers with tube- or trumpet-like petals. Such flowers are easy to explore for nectar with the birds' long beaks.

Not a Singer

Hummingbirds aren't songbirds. Their main sound is a kind of metallic *cheep-cheep-cheep*. But the noise can get quite loud and lively, especially when a feeding bird is telling another hungry hummer to go away.

Just Me, Myself, and I

Except for the brief mating season, individual hummingbirds live mostly solitary lives. The same holds for their long migration trips: Hummingbirds do not migrate in flocks. Rather, it's each bird for itself. Scientists think that by flying solo, the birds are less noticeable (and therefore safer from predators) than if they flew in large flocks.

More Than a Few Days

The migration trips of hummingbirds can cover more than 1,500 miles. The long trip of a ruby-throated hummer is filled with numerous stops for food and rest, and it takes many weeks. And there's more! After it arrives in Florida, it usually crosses the Gulf of Mexico (a distance of about five hundred miles) in a single nonstop flight that lasts around twenty-four hours. Sometimes the hummers avoid crossing the Gulf waters by flying around the Gulf over land.

How Do They Know When and Where to Go?

Some scientists believe that hummingbirds are very sensitive to changes in daylight, letting them know that winter is coming. Others believe that a chemical change in the bird's body suggests it's time to go. But at the moment, no one knows for sure.

Feisty Hummingbirds Defend Their Territory

Hummingbirds are tiny, but they can become aggressive fighters. Often the birds fight to protect a feeding site. Most fights end in one or more birds flying away, but a hummingbird's long, pointed beak can still inflict injury.

How to Become a Member of the Hummingbird Helper Club

The first thing to know and remember is this: Don't try to capture or even touch a hummingbird. They are small, delicate creatures and can easily be injured if handled. Just look. The tiny bird's "dance" in the air is simply wonderful to watch.

But there are still things you can do to make your yard a special hummingbird dining spot:

⟩ Plant a variety of flowers. It's the bright color that counts, because hummingbirds are attracted to vivid hues. They feed on the nectar contained in the flower's center. Plant flowers with wide petals—like flags waving to hummingbirds—that say, "Eat here!" Once hummingbirds find your tasty flowers, they will come back often. They have good memories of where they have eaten before.

⟩ Place a hummingbird feeder anywhere in your yard, even near a window. Feeders come in all shapes and sizes. Fill the feeder with nectar, which you can buy at a pet store. Soon you'll have a hummingbird show right before your eyes!

⟩ You can check out books or online sources that show you how to make your own feeder using old bottles or other objects around your house. You can even make your own nectar by following this easy recipe (or others you find in books or online):
Boil four cups of water and add one cup of white granulated sugar. Stir. Boil for two more minutes. After it cools, pour the liquid into your hummingbird feeder. Keep watching and you'll see visitors!

⟩ Many books and websites contain intriguing information about hummingbird life. Here are just a few of them:

The Hummingbird Book
Donald & Lillian Stokes
Little, Brown and Company, 2014

Hummingbirds
Ronald Orenstein
Firefly Books, 2014

Hummingbirds:
A Life-size Guide to Every Species
Michael Fogden, Marianne Taylor,
and Sheri L. Williamson
Harper Design, 2014

A Hummingbird in My House: The Story of Squeak
Arnette Heidcamp
The Crown Publishing Group, 1991

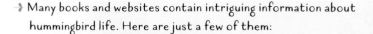

The author especially recommends one online source that contains well-organized information about hummingbirds: worldofhummingbirds.com. The site is divided into many small and easy-to-understand sections that cover every aspect of hummingbird life.

Happy hummingbirding!

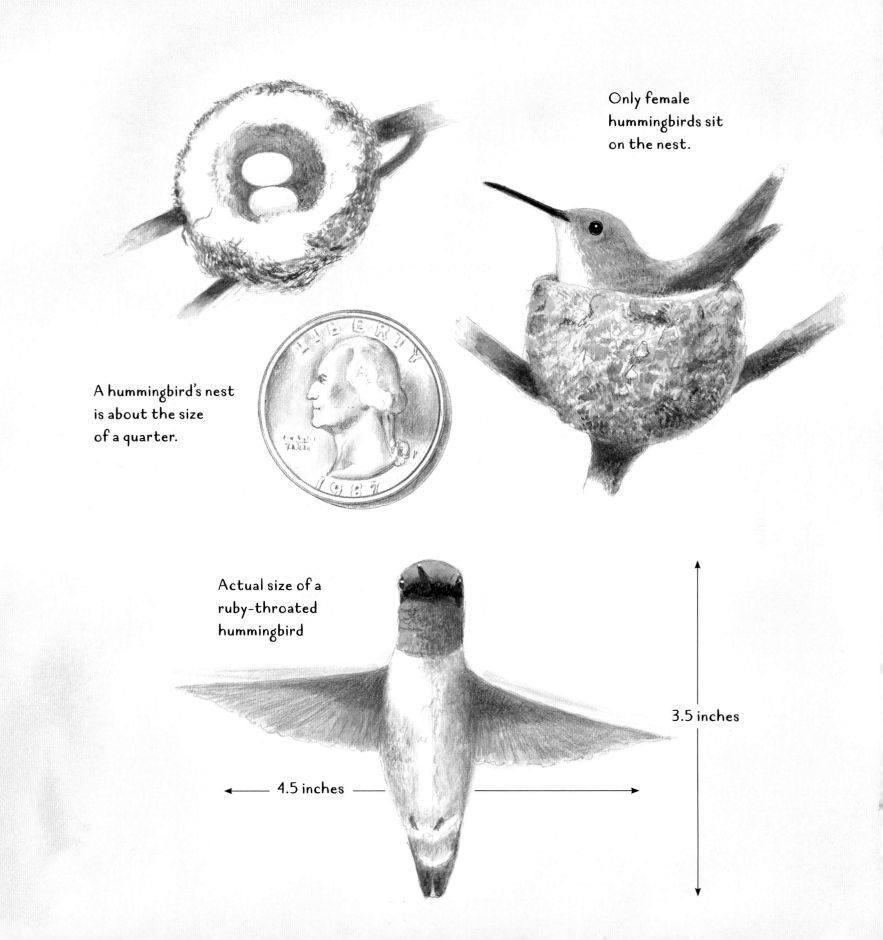

Only female
hummingbirds sit
on the nest.

A hummingbird's nest
is about the size
of a quarter.

Actual size of a
ruby-throated
hummingbird

3.5 inches

4.5 inches